# VENUE AND SEAT DISPUTE IN ARBITRATION

## VOLUME 2, ISSUE 4 OF BRILLOPEDIA

JAI ADITYA DUBEY

Made with ♥ on the Notion Press Platform
www.notionpress.com

# Contents


*Preface*      *v*

*Author*      *vii*

1. Abstract      1
2. Introduction      2
3. Statement Of Problem      3
4. Literature Review      4
5. Hypothesis      5
6. Research Methodology      6
7. What Is Meant By The Term 'seat' And The Term 'venue'      7
8. Only Venue Of Arbitration Mentioned In The Agreement      8
9. Recent Developments On This Issue      9
10. When The Agreement Is Completely Silent On Place, Venue, Or Seat Of Arbitration      11
11. Conclusion      13

# Preface

"Start writing, no matter what. The water does not flow until the faucet is turned on".

- Louis L'Amour

Hundreds of students and professors are contributing their work to Brillopedia, we are here to provide ample information about Law and Contemporary issues. Our aim is to provide a platform for today's generation to express their views and ideas on law and contemporary law.

# Author

Jai Aditya Dubey

CHAPTER ONE

# ABSTRACT

Arbitration in India is governed by the arbitration and conciliation act of 1996. Arbitration and conciliation are one of the most practiced modes of dispute resolution methods being followed in India as through these modes of dispute resolution people can settle their disputes as soon as possible, moreover,these methods are more cost-effective modes of dispute resolution.

As one of the most used methods of dispute resolution in the country, it has suffered some legal issues out of which was the issue of seat and venue of arbitration which had evolved by various judgments of the supreme court through a plethora of judgments given through various cases. In arbitration, venue refers to the place where arbitration would be conducted whereas seat refers to the area of jurisdiction of the arbitration as to which area courts would have the jurisdiction to hear if any disputes arise out of that dispute arises out of that arbitration.

Going through the statutory law of the country section 20 of the arbitration and conciliation act of 1996 talks about the seat and venue of arbitration but there are no terms for seat and venue in the statutory law itself instead the act talks about the place of arbitration, the term mentioned in the act is 'seat of arbitration', but the act does not differentiate between seat and venue so the courts in India decide the cases related to seat and venue on the basis of the precedent set by the honorable supreme court of India through various judgments given through various cases.

# CHAPTER TWO

# INTRODUCTION

The issue of venue and seat of arbitration came under the scrutiny of the supreme court of the country when the parties to the dispute started challenging the jurisdiction of the court to hear that particular issue related to arbitration. These issues get invoked when parties fail to mention a clause or agreement in the contract itself mentioning the venue and seat of arbitration, challenging the jurisdiction of the court to hear the issue related to arbitration is used as a defense by one of the parties. In some of the cases, the parties do mention the venue of arbitration but fail to mention the seat of arbitration there is the issue of whether the venue of arbitration can be the seat of arbitration or not. In one of the cases of the supreme court, the court had to face the issue to decide whether can venue be seat when there are multiple venues of arbitration. Moreover, in one of the recent case of Inox renewables vs Harvey electricals in 2021 the supreme court of India dealt with the issue that whether the venue of arbitration can be changed by mutual consent of both parties of the arbitration.

CHAPTER THREE

# STATEMENT OF PROBLEM

This paper mainly talks about the issue of seat and venue of arbitration in India as the statutory law governing arbitration in the country is silent on this, this issue was settled by the honorable supreme court of India through various judgments. The issue in this research paper mainly revolves around determining the jurisdictional seat of arbitration when the arbitration clause mentioned in the contract is completely silent on that.

# CHAPTER FOUR

# LITERATURE REVIEW

1.  **P C Markanda Arbitration - Step by Step**

This book helps the researcher to go through the various nuances of arbitration and understand the basics of arbitration. This book helps the researcher to go through different issues related to arbitration and go through various judgments of the past given by the honorable supreme court of India and various state high courts in India[1].

**2. THE ARBITRATION AND CONCILIATION ACT, 1996**

This bare act helps the researcher to go through the statutory law of the country, as mentioned and drafted in the arbitration and conciliation act of 1996[2].

**RESEARCH OBJECTIVE**

1.  The objective of this research paper is to go through the nuances of the issue related to arbitration which concerns the venue and jurisdictional seat of Arbitration

2.  The main focus of the research is to highlight how this issue was settled by the honorable supreme court of India through a plethora of judgments.

3.  The next objective of this research paper is to highlight the recent developments in this issue which can act as a precedent in future cases.

[1] P C Markanda Arbitration - Step by Step
[2]THE ARBITRATION AND CONCILIATION ACT, 1996

# CHAPTER FIVE

# HYPOTHESIS

The arbitration and conciliation act of 1996 is completely silent on the topic of the venue and seat of arbitration, section 20 of the arbitration and conciliation act states the term "place of arbitration" in the act itself, therefore issues like when the arbitration clause is silent on the seat of arbitration is it valid to consider the venue of arbitration as the seat of arbitration or when can the venue be the seat of arbitration and when the arbitration clause is completely silent on the seat, venue or place of arbitration, then will the arbitrator have the power to fix the seat of arbitration. These issues were settled by the supreme court in cases like BALCO vs Kaiser aluminum, BGS SGS Soma Vs NHPC, Inox renewables Vs Harvey electricals, etc

# CHAPTER SIX

# RESEARCH METHODOLOGY

The research methodology which is used by the researcher is doctrinal research, the researcher of this research paper had gone through books, articles as well as various judgments given by the honorable supreme court of India and various state high courts of the country. This topic became aninteresting topic of the researcher while working as an intern at an arbitration firm, Markanda Advocates. Working as an intern going through various case laws has helped me understand the nuances of arbitration and find this an interesting topic of research.

# CHAPTER SEVEN

# WHAT IS MEANT BY THE TERM 'SEAT' AND THE TERM 'VENUE'

According to the statutory law of the country section 20 of the arbitration and conciliation act of 1996,there is no such term as seat or venue mentioned in the act itself, the act only states about 'place of arbitration'. The act is itself silent on the terms seat of arbitration and venue of arbitration. This issue was for the first time viewed by the supreme court of India in the year 2002 in the case of Bhatia International Vs Bulk Trading SA in this case the appellant had filed an application under section 62 of the Arbitration and conciliation act in the district court of MP Indore held that the appellant raised that the application is not maintainable since foreign awards are not binding in India[1]. However the judgment of Bhatia International vs bulk trading SA was overruled by the supreme court of India in the case of Balco vs Kaiser aluminum in the year 2012, in this case, arbitration took place in England the award was rendered in England the award was rendered by the arbitrator was set aside by the district court as the award was rendered outside India, the decision of the district court was challenged and the supreme court of India the supreme court in this case held that a claim can be made to enforce the award in India even though the seat of arbitration is not in India, therefore awards rendered by foreign arbitrations can be made enforceable in the country[2].

[1] Bhatia International v. Bulk Trading S.A., (2002) 4 SCC 105

[2] Bharat Aluminium Co. v. Kaiser Aluminium Technical Services Inc., (2012) 9 SCC 552

# CHAPTER EIGHT

# ONLY VENUE OF ARBITRATION MENTIONED IN THE AGREEMENT

When arbitration takes place the seat of arbitration determines the place of jurisdiction of that arbitration as to which area courts would have the power to review the matter if there is any issue related to that arbitration, some times the parties to the arbitration fail to mention the seat of arbitration whereas they do mention the venue of arbitration, one of the parties to arbitration take it as a defense in the court that mentioning of the venue of arbitration would not amount to the venue being the seat of arbitration. This issue reached the supreme court of India in the case of Roger Shashova Vs Mukesh Sharma the supreme court of India held that when the seat of arbitration is not mentioned in the arbitration agreement then it becomes safe to conclude that the venue of arbitration should be the seat of arbitration[1]. Therefore, through this judgment, the supreme court contended that if the seat of arbitration has not been mentioned in the arbitration agreement, then the venue of the arbitration could be considered the seat of arbitration,and the courts in that venue would have the jurisdiction to hear any dispute arising out of that arbitration. The same was enumerated by the supreme court of India in the case of BGS SGS Soma JV Vs NHPC in this casethe honorable supreme court propounded a test and laid down that when a particular place is designated as the venue of arbitration the same should be considered to be the seat of arbitration[2].

[1]Roger Shashoua v. Mukesh Sharma, (2017) 14 SCC 722

[2] BGS SGS SOMA JV v. NHPC, (2020) 4 SCC 234

# CHAPTER NINE

# RECENT DEVELOPMENTS ON THIS ISSUE

In recent years the issue of the seat and venue of arbitration had gone through the scrutiny of the supreme court of India. In one of the recent cases in the year 2020 the case of MankastuImpex private limited VsAirvisual Limited, the honorable supreme court of India viewed the issue that if both the terms venue and seat are missing from the arbitration agreement and the only term present is "place of arbitration" then it won't amount seat or venue of arbitration, in this case, the term stated in the contract was that the seat of arbitration would be Hong Kong whereas one of the clauses in the arbitration agreement stated that this MoU is governed by the laws of India, without regard to its conflicts of laws provisions and courts at New Delhi shall have the jurisdiction. Therefore the court in this case held that in case of the term seat and venue missing in the arbitration agreement and the mere presence of the term "place of arbitration" would not amount to the seat of arbitration[1].

The second issue which was recently viewed by the supreme court of India was whether the venue of arbitration could be changed by mutual consent between the parties this issue was addressed by the honorable supreme court of India in the case of Inox renewables Vs Harvey electricals the issue. in this case, was that the parties to the arbitration had chosen Jaipur as the venue of arbitration, later the venue of arbitration was changed from Jaipur to Ahmedabad by mutual consent between the parties, later the award of arbitration was rendered in Ahmedabad and the award was rendered in favor of the respondent, further the award was challenged in the high court of Ahmedabad. The petitioner claimed that since the arbitration took place in Ahmedabad therefore the High court of Ahmedabad would have the jurisdiction to hear the matter but later the respondent contended the jurisdiction of the Ahmedabad High court, latter this issue went to the honorable supreme court of India through a special leave petition. Where the supreme court allowed the petition in Ahmedabad High court.

The court through this judgment contended that: -

1. Venue of arbitration can be the seat of arbitration
2. Transfer of venue can take place by mutual consent[2]

[1]MankastuImpex (P) Ltd. v. Airvisual Ltd., (2020) 5 SCC 399

[2]Inox Renewables Ltd. v. Jayesh Electricals Ltd., 2021 SCC OnLine SC 448

# WHEN THE AGREEMENT IS COMPLETELY SILENT ON PLACE, VENUE, OR SEAT OF ARBITRATION

In one of the recent cases of 2022 the honorable supreme court of India in the case of BBR (INDIA) PRIVATE LIMITED Vs. S.P. SINGLA CONSTRUCTION PRIVATE LIMITED, the honorable supreme court reviewed the issue that when the arbitration clause is completely silent and does not stipulate the seat or venue of arbitration. In this case, the issue that came before the honorable supreme court was that the contract's arbitration clause was completely silent on the venue, seat, or place of arbitration. The first arbitration proceedings took place in Panchkula, Haryana and neither party objected to the place of arbitration as fixed by the arbitral tribunal further proceedings were conducted in Chandigarh, and later on, the venue was shifted to Delhi. Once the arbitral award was rendered, the award got challenged and the issue of jurisdiction arose the appellant, in this case, had applied before the high court of Delhi under section 34 of the act after the arbitral tribunal, the honorable supreme court, in this case, observed that the seat of arbitration was fixed by the arbitrator under section 20(2) of the act (Panchkula, Haryana) and therefore courts in Delhi do not have the jurisdiction to hear this matter. Through this judgment, the honorable supreme court of India held that the arbitrator has the power to fix the seat of the arbitration under section 42 of the arbitration and conciliation act of 1996[1]

[1] BBR (India) (P) Ltd. v. S.P. Singla Constructions (P) Ltd., 2022 SCC OnLine SC 642

# CHAPTER ELEVEN

# CONCLUSION

The issue of seat and venue was settled by the supreme court of India through a plethora of judgements, the issue of seat not mentioned in arbitration clause was settled through a plethora of judgements. The statutory law of arbitration being completely silent of the issue, the honorable supreme court of India has set a precedent for future references. However, after these issues people entering into arbitration agreement make sure that while entering into contract they do mention the venue and seat of arbitration within arbitration agreement. After these set precedents the courts at lower level get a set pattern to look forward towards future issues.

www.ingramcontent.com/pod-product-compliance
Lightning Source LLC
Chambersburg PA
CBHW071259140726
47996CB00007B/2913